PS130553 DISK 4

To

Coventry City Council

EXTREME

Space Tourist
A Traveller's Guide to the Solar System

Stuart Atkinson

A & C Black • London

Produced for A & C Black by

Monkey Puzzle Media Ltd
The Rectory, Eyke, Woodbridge
Suffolk IP12 2QW, UK

Published by A & C Black Publishers Limited
38 Soho Square, London W1D 3HB

First published 2008
Copyright © 2008 A & C Black Publishers Limited

ISBN 978-1-4081-0031-8 (hardback)
ISBN 978-1-4081-0123-0 (paperback)

Editor: Steve Parker
Design: Mayer Media Ltd
Picture research: Lynda Lines
Series consultant: Jane Turner

This book is produced using paper that is made
from wood grown in managed, sustainable forests.
It is natural, renewable and recyclable. The logging
and manufacturing processes conform to the
environmental regulations of the country of origin.

Printed in China by C & C Offset Printing Co., Ltd

Picture acknowledgements
Corbis p. 25 bottom (Bettmann); Getty Images pp.
14 top and 15 top (NASA-JPL-Caltech/Science
Faction), 28 (AFP); MPM Images pp. 7 (Digital
Vision), 13 (Digital Vision); NASA pp. 6–7, 8, 9, 11,
12, 14 bottom, 15 bottom (Pat Rawlings), 19, 21,
23, 24–25, 25 top, 27; PA Photos p. 16 (AP); Rex
Features p. 5; Science Photo Library pp. 1 (Chris
Butler), 4 (Victor Habbick Visions), 10 (Christian
Darkin), 17 (Roger Harris), 18 (Detlev van
Ravenswaay), 20 (Chris Butler), 22–23 (David A
Hardy, Futures: 50 Years in Space), 26 (Robert
McNaught), 29 (Victor Habbick Visions).

The front cover shows an artist's impression of
astronauts on the surface of Mars (Getty Images/
James Porto).

Every effort has been made to contact copyright
holders of material reproduced in this book. Any
omissions will be rectified in subsequent printings if
notice is given to the publishers.

CONTENTS

Abbreviations **m** stands for metres • **ft** stands for feet • **in** stands for inches • **cm** stands for centimetres • **km** stands for kilometres

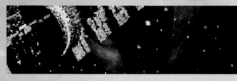

Leaving Earth

Where have you been on holiday? Perhaps a different town, another country or even across a continent? Tourists of the future might go still further. Imagine going on a sightseeing tour of the **Solar System**!

The Solar System is the Sun and everything that goes around it. It has eight large **planets**, including our Earth, plus hundreds of smaller **moons** and thousands of other objects. So there'd be lots of exciting sights to see.

If you went on a space holiday, where could you go and what could you do? Let's find out!

*Imagine spending part of your tour in a space hotel like the one in this artist's impression. But you'd need a **spacesuit** to go outside!*

Space-Speak

An object travelling around another object in space is said to **orbit** it. Earth orbits the Sun. If you flew up into space, you would orbit the Earth.

planet a Solar System object that's roughly round and is the largest in its area of space

Solar panels turn sunlight into electricity for the bus's equipment — including life support!

All aboard! An artist's impression of a space tour bus. From 1,000 km (625 miles) above Earth, the views are stunning!

Powerful **rocket** engines blast the tour bus into space.

Wings don't work in space as there's no air. But they are needed for takeoff and landing.

Large portholes (windows) let you see stunning views.

rocket a powerful machine that carries things into space

On the Moon

The Moon is the first stop on your tour. It's only a three-day space flight away from Earth.

When astronauts first landed on the Moon in 1969 they found ash-grey dust, shattered **boulders** and bowl-shaped craters. Standing on the Moon you'd see hills and grey plains all around, with Earth shining above like a blue-and-white marble. Because there is no air to make the Moon's sky blue, it's as black as coal. Also the Moon's gravity is weaker than Earth's. So you'd bounce instead of walk, and leap around like a kangaroo!

Imagine stepping off your tour bus here! The Moon has no air or water. Without a spacesuit you'd be dead in seconds!

Low mountains in the background.

Much of the surface is covered in grey dust.

This low hill formed billions of years ago when the Moon had **volcanoes**.

boulders very large pieces of rock or stone

*Second person on the Moon was Buzz Aldrin. Because there's no **atmosphere** or weather there, his boot-prints in the dust will last for millions of years.*

Space-Speak

The Moon orbits the Earth every 28 days. The sunlit part we see from Earth appears to change shape, from new Moon to full Moon.

The **lunar** rover, an electric buggy, is still there on the Moon's surface.

Astronaut Eugene Cernan gathers some Moon rocks to take back home.

atmosphere layers of gas surrounding a space object like a planet or moon

Sun at the centre

After the Moon, your exciting tour of the Solar System would head for its centre – the Sun.

Sunspots are always changing. They grow over a few weeks, then fade away as new ones appear elsewhere. Even a small sunspot is bigger than the whole Earth.

The Sun is a **star**, like all the other stars that twinkle in the night sky. But because it's the closest star to Earth – only 146 million kilometres (92 million miles) away – it looks like a huge ball of fire. (Never look at the Sun through binoculars or a **telescope**, or even without them. You could go blind!) The Sun is so bright because it's incredibly hot. Its surface temperature is 6,000 degrees Celsius (10,800 degrees Fahrenheit), over 30 times hotter than a home oven.

star huge ball of flaming gases in space

Make sure you take pictures of ...

... Sunspots. These are enormous magnetic storms dotted about on the surface of the Sun.

This huge loop of flames is a solar prominence, hundreds of times bigger than Earth.

Sunspots are cooler, darker patches.

The Sun is 109 times **WIDER** than Earth.

The surface is so hot, it would burn you to a crisp even if you were 10 million km (6.2 million miles) away.

The Sun's volume is so huge, more than a million Earths could fit inside.

telescope makes faraway things look nearer

Mercury's furnace

Tiny Mercury is the closest planet to the Sun. It whizzes around the Sun once every 88 Earth days, which is one Mercury year. If you lived there you'd have a birthday every 88 days!

Mercury's surface is covered with huge bowl-like craters, cliffs and canyons. The gigantic Caloris Basin crater formed when a piece of space rock 150 km (95 miles) wide hit the planet.

Because Mercury is so close to the Sun, it's like a furnace. On the surface it's ten times hotter than in an oven. Yet there may be ice in deep craters near Mercury's poles, at the planet's top and bottom, where the Sun's rays cannot reach.

day time taken for an object like a planet to rotate once

Make sure you take pictures of ...

... Mercury's huge steep cliffs, which are known as rupes. Discovery Rupes is 650 kilometres (400 miles) long, one and a half times the size of Earth's Grand Canyon.

Mercury is so bare, rocky and crater-ridden, you might mistake it for Earth's Moon.

Mercury takes 60 of our Earth days to turn around once. That time is one Mercury day.

Since a Mercury day is 60 Earth days, and a Mercury year is 88 Earth days, this planet's day is almost three-quarters as long as its year!

Almost all of Mercury's atmosphere has been blasted away by the Sun's incredible heat.

year time taken for an object to travel once around the Sun

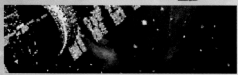

Shining Venus

Venus is often visible in the night sky from Earth. When it shines brightly after sunset, it's known as the Evening Star.

Space probes use special radar equipment to see through Venus' clouds to the surface mountains and valleys. The peak on the right is Gula Mons, one-third as high as Earth's Mount Everest

Next planet out from the Sun after Mercury is Venus. It's named after the Roman goddess of love because it shines so beautifully when seen from Earth. This is because its clouds reflect the Sun's rays like a mirror. Many surface features of Venus are also named after famous women from legend and history, such as King Arthur's queen Guinevere and Greek goddess Aphrodite. But when you reach Venus you'd find it's far from beautiful. It's an ugly, deadly place!

Take pictures of ...

... Venera 7, the first space probe to land on Venus in 1970. Or what's left of it – the acid fumes of Venus's atmosphere may have eaten it all away!

space probe an unmanned spacecraft sent to study objects out in space

Thick clouds of poison gas would choke you, and you'd never see the Sun through them.

Under the clouds, the surface of Venus is made of orange-brown rocks.

Storms rage in the gloomy yellow sky.

The Aphrodite Terra highlands are a major landmark.

The surface temperature on Venus is 460°C (860°F), almost hot enough to melt your **spacesuit**!

spacesuit special protective clothing to keep astronauts alive in space

Mars, Red Planet

Mars is nicknamed the Red Planet because it looks bright red when seen from Earth. When you arrive, you'd see that its rocky surface really is reddy-brown – because it's made of rust!

The rocks and dust on Mars contain lots of iron oxide, the same substance that's in rust. Mars is only half Earth's size, but it has some gigantic craters, canyons and mountains. Olympus Mons is three times higher than Mount Everest. If Mariner Valley was on Earth, it would stretch across the United States of America!

Long ago Mars had rivers, lakes and possibly oceans, but now it's very dry. This is the edge of the 750-m (2,500-ft) wide Victoria Crater.

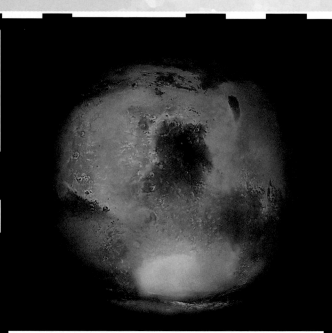

Deadly!

The Martian atmosphere contains poisonous carbon dioxide and methane gases.

Mars changes with the seasons. The pictures opposite and below show the two sides of the planet in late summer, with a pale ice cap at the South Pole (bottom). In winter the ice caps at both poles grow.

Mars is farther from the Sun than Earth and so it's very cold, down to minus 130 degrees Celsius (minus 266 degrees Fahrenheit). Whirling winds and dust storms swirl across the plains. Many scientists believe simple forms of life could live under the surface. Have a look if you go!

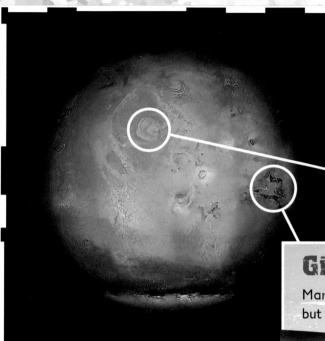

Massive!

Olympus Mons, an old **volcano**, is the largest mountain in the whole Solar System.

Gigantic!

Mariner Valley is like Earth's Grand Canyon, but three times deeper and 10 times longer!

Make sure you take pictures of ...

... the Vikings on Mars. But they're not warriors from Norway, they're space probes that landed in 1976.

Hi, everyone at home! Astronauts may get to Mars by 2037.

volcano an opening in a planet's crust through which gases, dust and other substances erupt

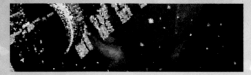

Asteroids everywhere

After Mars, the next stop on your tour is the Asteroid Belt. Here you'll see thousands of rocky lumps called asteroids.

The Japanese space probe Hayabusa photographed large boulders on the asteroid Itokawa.

Asteroids are leftovers from when the Solar System formed, nearly five billion years ago. They orbit the Sun like miniature planets, and are basically pieces of a world that never formed. Flying past one, you'd see a huge chunk of stone, or metal, or a mixture of both.

Astronomers keep a close watch for any asteroids passing close to Earth. If one hit us, we could become as extinct as the dinosaurs.

astronomers people who study space and the universe

Many asteroids are covered in craters and hills. Some even have their own tiny moons.

An asteroid's **gravity** is so weak, you'd have to tie yourself down or you'd float away!

The biggest asteroids are hundreds of kilometres across.

Hopefully Earthlings have spotted this asteroid and know it will just miss their planet!

Space-Speak

The largest asteroid was Ceres, named after the Sicilian Goddess of Grain. But Ceres is now called a dwarf planet, and the largest asteroid is Pallas.

gravity the pulling force between any two objects

Jupiter, King of Planets

You couldn't land on Jupiter because it has no hard, firm surface to land on!

Jupiter is the biggest planet, a **gas giant** made of gases and liquids. From Earth it looks like a bright yellow-blue star, but from your spaceship window, you'd see a huge globe with bands of brown and orange clouds.

Jupiter has more than 60 moons. It also has rings of dust, but these are so dark, they'd be hard to see from your spaceship.

Jupiter looms huge over the horizon, in this view from its moon Io. Volcanoes on Io pour out gas and fumes. Some astronomers think there might be **alien** *life beneath the frozen surface of another Jupiter moon, Europa.*

alien not from or to do with Earth

Further information

Activities

- If there's an observatory where you live, ask to go there and talk to the astronomers about the Solar System, and maybe look through the telescope.

- Check if your local museum or exhibition centre has any exhibits or talks about space.

- Find out if your town has an astronomical society. You can go to their meetings to learn a lot more about planets and space exploration.

Websites

www.aas.org
The American Astronomical Society aims to further the science of astronomy and improve astronomy education.

http://planetary.org/home
The Planetary Society inspires people through education, research and participation, to explore other worlds and seek other life.

www.popastro.com
The Society for Popular Astronomy is Britain's largest astronomical society for amateur astronomers.

www.britastro.org/baa
The British Astronomical Association works to promote general interest in astronomy for beginners as well as experts.

http://amazing-space.stsci.edu
The Hubble Space Telescope kids' website.

http://solarsystem.nasa.gov/kids/index.cfm
NASA's solar system guide for young people.

www.enchantedlearning.com/subjects/astronomy
Enchanted Learning's space section.

Films

Blue Planet directed by Ben Burtt (IMAX, 1993) Amazing images of the Earth from space as seen by space shuttle astronauts.

The Dream Is Alive directed by Graeme Ferguson (IMAX, 1985) How astronauts live and work in space.

Apollo 13 directed by Ron Howard (MCA/Universal Pictures, 1995) One of the best space movies, telling the amazing true story of the unlucky Apollo 13 Moon mission.

Index